SandCastle™

The Alphabet

D0003998

Zz

Kelly Doudna

ABDO
Publishing Company

Published by SandCastle™, an imprint of ABDO Publishing Company, 8000 West 78th Street, Edina, Minnesota 55435.

Printed in the United States, North Mankato, Minnesota.

Cover and interior photo credits: ArtToday, Comstock, Digital Stock, Digital Vision, Eyewire, PhotoDisc

012000
112012

Library of Congress Cataloging-in-Publication Data

Doudna, Kelly, 1963-
    Zz / Kelly Doudna.
       p. cm. -- (The alphabet)
       ISBN 1-57765-446-3 (hardcover)
       ISBN 1-59197-026-1 (paperback)
       1. Readers (Primary) [1. Readers] I. Title.

PE1119 .D68694 2000
428.1--dc21
                                              00-056904

The SandCastle concept, content, and reading method have been reviewed and approved by a national advisory board including literacy specialists, librarians, elementary school teachers, early childhood education professionals, and parents.

Let Us Know

After reading the book, SandCastle would like you to tell us your stories about reading. What is your favorite page? Was there something hard that you needed help with? Share the ups and downs of learning to read. We want to hear from you! To get posted on the ABDO Publishing Company Web site, send us email at:

sandcastle@abdopub.com

About SandCastle™

A professional team of educators, reading specialists, and content developers created the SandCastle™ series to support young readers as they develop reading skills and strategies and increase their general knowledge. The SandCastle™ series has four levels that correspond to early literacy development in young children. The levels are provided to help teachers and parents select the appropriate books for young readers.

Emerging Readers
(no flags)

Beginning Readers
(1 flag)

Transitional Readers
(2 flags)

Fluent Readers
(3 flags)

These levels are meant only as a guide. All levels are subject to change.

To see a complete list of SandCastle™ books and other nonfiction titles from ABDO Publishing Company, visit **www.abdopub.com** or contact us at:
4940 Viking Drive, Edina, Minnesota 55435 • 1-800-800-1312 • fax: 1-952-831-1632

Liza has fun with Liz.

Lizzy has a crazy hat.

Izzy stands in the drizzle.

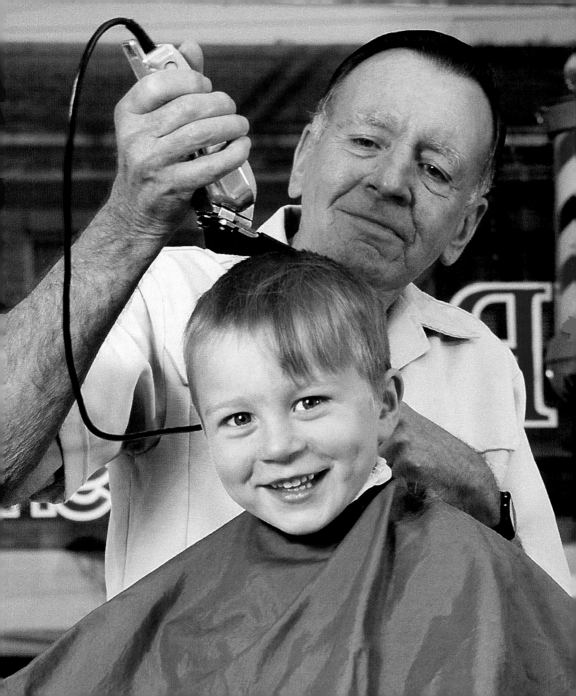

Ozzy gets a buzz cut.

Our tent is cozy.

Zach zips along on skates.

Zubin has a fuzzy bunny.

Suzu eats a frozen treat.

What does Suzie have?

(puzzle)

Words I Can Read

Nouns

A noun is a person, place, or thing

bunny (BUHN-ee) p. 17
cut (KUHT) p. 11
drizzle (DRIZ-uhl) p. 9
fun (FUHN) p. 5
hat (HAT) p. 7
puzzle (PUHZ-uhl) p. 21
skates (SKAYTSS) p. 15
tent (TENT) p. 13
treat (TREET) p. 19

Proper Nouns

A proper noun is the name
of a person, place, or thing

Izzy (IZ-ee) p. 9
Liz (LIZ) p. 5
Liza (LIZE-uh) p. 5
Lizzy (LIZ-ee) p. 7

Verbs

A verb is an action or being word

More Zz Words

lizard

zebra

zigzag

zipper

24